I'm Not Scared

Written by Kirsten Hall

Illustrated by Joan Holub

My First
READER

SCHOLASTIC INC.

New York Toronto London Auckland Sydney
Mexico City New Delhi Hong Kong Buenos Aires

ISBN 0-516-24496-5

12 11 10 9 8 7 6 5 4 3 2 1   3 4 5 6 7 8/0

Printed in the U.S.A.   61

First Scholastic printing, September 2003

Note to Parents and Teachers

Once a reader can recognize and identify the 32 words
used to tell this story, he or she will be able to read successfully
the entire book. These 32 words are repeated throughout the story,
so that young readers will be able to easily recognize
the words and understand their meaning.

The 32 words used in this book are:

a	high	of	the
are	I'm	outside	trees
at	in	owls	we
bumblebees	lakes	scared	what
call	light	should	when
climbing	night	sky	who
do	not	snakes	without
giant	now	swinging	you

I'm not scared of climbing trees.

I'm not scared of bumblebees.

I'm not scared of swinging high.

Now I'm swinging in the sky!

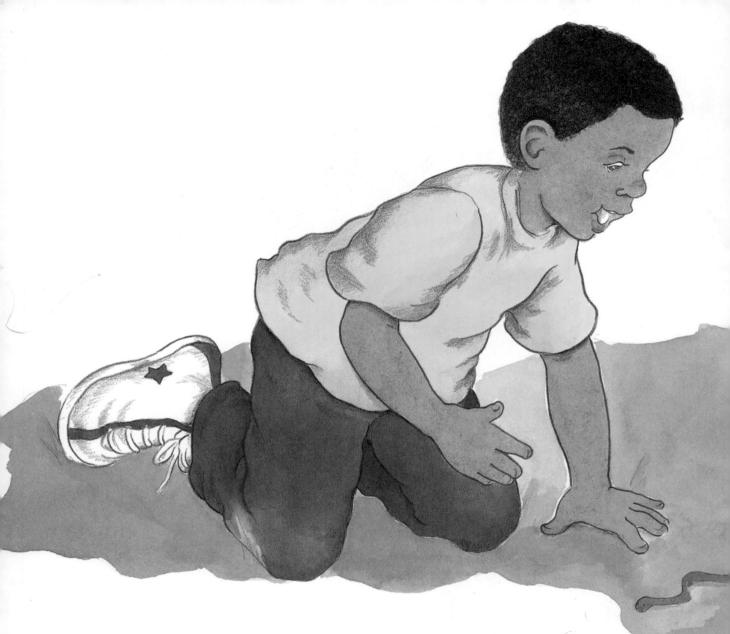

I'm not scared of giant snakes.

I'm not scared of snakes in lakes.

I'm not scared outside at night.

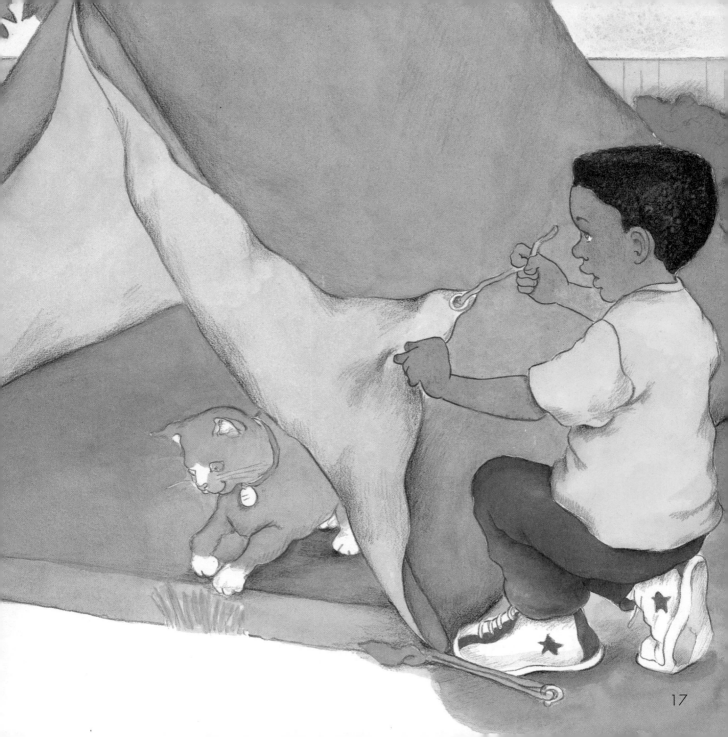

17

I'm not scared without a light.

I'm not scared when owls call who.

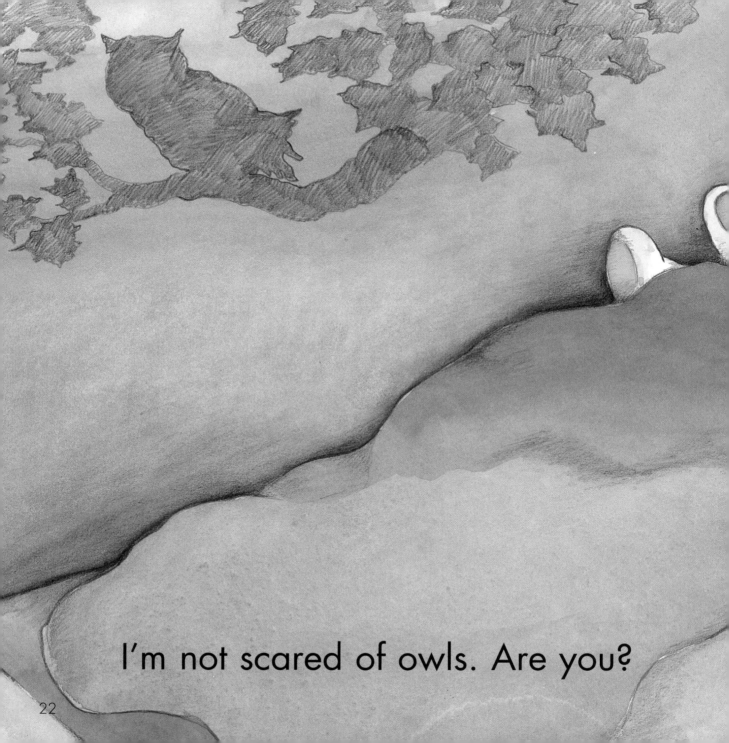

I'm not scared of owls. Are you?

WHOOOOOOOOOOOOO!

Now I'm scared. I'm scared.

Are you?

Now I'm scared!

What should we do?

ABOUT THE AUTHOR

Kirsten Hall has lived most of her life in New York City. While she was still in high school, she published her first book for children, *Bunny, Bunny*. Since then, she has written and published more than sixty children's books. A former early education teacher, Kirsten currently works as a children's book editor.

ABOUT THE ILLUSTRATOR

Joan Holub was born in Houston, Texas. She graduated with a BFA from the University of Texas and began her career as an illustrator of books for children while she lived and worked in New York City. Her hobbies are hiking, bicycle riding, and reading. Holub now lives in Seattle, Washington, with her husband, George, and two cats, Boo and Scout.